Looking at Literature

Charlotte Guillain

heinemann
raintree

© 2015 Heinemann Raintree
an imprint of Capstone Global Library, LLC
Chicago, Illinois

To contact Capstone Global Library, please call 800-747-4992, or visit our web site www.capstonepub.com

All rights reserved. No part of this publication may be reproduced or transmitted in any form or by any means, electronic or mechanical, including photocopying, recording, taping, or any information storage and retrieval system, without permission in writing from the publisher.

Edited by Clare Lewis and Holly Beaumont
Designed by Philippa Jenkins
Picture research by Wanda Winch
Originated by Capstone Global Library Ltd
Produced by Helen McCreath
Printed and Bound in China by CTPS

18 17 16 15 14
10 9 8 7 6 5 4 3 2 1

Library of Congress Cataloging-in-Publication Data
Guillain, Charlotte.
  Looking at literature / Charlotte Guillain.
      pages cm.—(Connect with text)
  Includes bibliographical references and index.
  ISBN 978-1-4109-6831-9 (pb)
  1. Literature—History and criticism—Juvenile literature. 2. Literature—Authorship—Juvenile literature. I. Title.

PN45.G793 2015
801'.3—dc23   2014016450

This book has been officially leveled by using the F&P Text Level Gradient™ Leveling System.

Acknowledgments
The author and publisher are grateful to the following for permission to reproduce copyright material: ®Batman courtesy of ©DC Comics, 60; Alamy: Matthew Taylor, 20, Network Photographers, 14, Photostock-Israel/Chad Shahar, 28, Steven May, 21; AP Images: Elaine Thompson, 98, Harry Cabluck, 103; Atinuke, artist, 48; Capstone: Charles Barnett III and Phil Miller, 73, Daniel Ferran, 63, Dennis Calero, 72, Erik Lervold, 66, Fernando Luiz, 94, Gerardo Sandoval, 59, Jose Alfonso Ocampo Ruiz, 61, Josh Alves, 13, Peter McDonnell, 77, Richard Dominguez and Charles Barnett III, 76, Capstone Studio: Karon Dubke, 8, 17, 54, 56, 62, 67, 68, 69, 78, 79; Corbis: Bettmann, 91, Blue Lantern Studio, 53, Colin McPherson, 99, Matthias Tunger, 55, Reuters/Benoit Tessier, 74; Dreamstime: Diego Vito Cervo, 42; Getty Images Inc: Dave J. Hogan, 89, Gamma-Rapho/Marc Gantier, 71, Jeremy Sutton-Hibert, 101 (right), Mark G. Renders, 70, Neilson Barnard, 29, Redferns/Brigitte Engl, 102, SFX Magazine/Rob Monk, 64, The British Library/Robana, 87, The Image Bank/Cavan Images, 9, Timelapse Library Ltd./Tony Evans, 45; iStockphoto: 2thirdsphoto, 7, Duncan1890, 18, IndigoBetta, 43; Library of Congress: Prints and Photographs Division, 41, 46, 50, 88, 97; Newscom: Everett Collection, 86, Getty Images Inc: AFP/Peter Muhly, 49, picture-alliance/DPA/Jens Buettner, 16, picture-alliance/DPA/Oliver Berg, 15, Polaris/Stephanie Keith, 12, SIPA/Saez Pascal, 58, Zuma Press/Geoff Swaine, 47, Zuma Press/Ian Gavan, 22; Rex USA: c.Goldwyn/Everett, 65, Christopher Jones, 104, Geoffrey Swaine, 25, ITV, 96, Rex, 19, Rex/Heathcliff O'Malley, 26; Shutterstock: Aija Lehtonen, 85, andreiuc88, 38, Angela Harburn, 24, Antonia Gravante, 36, auremar, 93 (bottom), Carla Castagno, 51, deedl, 75, Dmitry Morgan, 11, Elena Schweitzer, 23, Eugene Ivanov, 83 (top), holbox, 39, Jacek Chabraszewski, 27, KUCO, 52, Michael C. Gray, 6, mykeyruna, 100, naluwan, 83 (bottom), Olesya Feketa, 95, Olga Popova, 44, Pakhyuscha, 84, PathDoc, 37, patjo, 93 (top), Pressmaster, 105, prudkov, 31, ririe, 101 (left), Samuel Borges Photography, 30, sunabesyou, 32, urfin, pencil, Vietrov Dmytro, 35, wavebreakmedia, 40.

Every effort has been made to contact copyright holders of any material reproduced in this book. Any omissions will be rectified in subsequent printings if notice is given to the publisher.

All the Internet addresses (URLs) given in this book were valid at the time of going to press. However, due to the dynamic nature of the Internet, some addresses may have changed, or sites may have changed or ceased to exist since publication. While the author and publisher regret any inconvenience this may cause readers, no responsibility for any such changes can be accepted by either the author or the publisher.

Contents

What Do You Like to Read?........................... 6
Want to Try Something New? 8

What Is a Novel? 10
Characters... 12
Plot 14
Voice and Tense 16
Adventure Stories 18
Funny Novels 20
Fantasy Novels... 22
Science Fiction 24
Mystery Stories 26
Realistic Stories 28
Finding the Right Novel for You 30
Take It Further.. 32

 Continued...

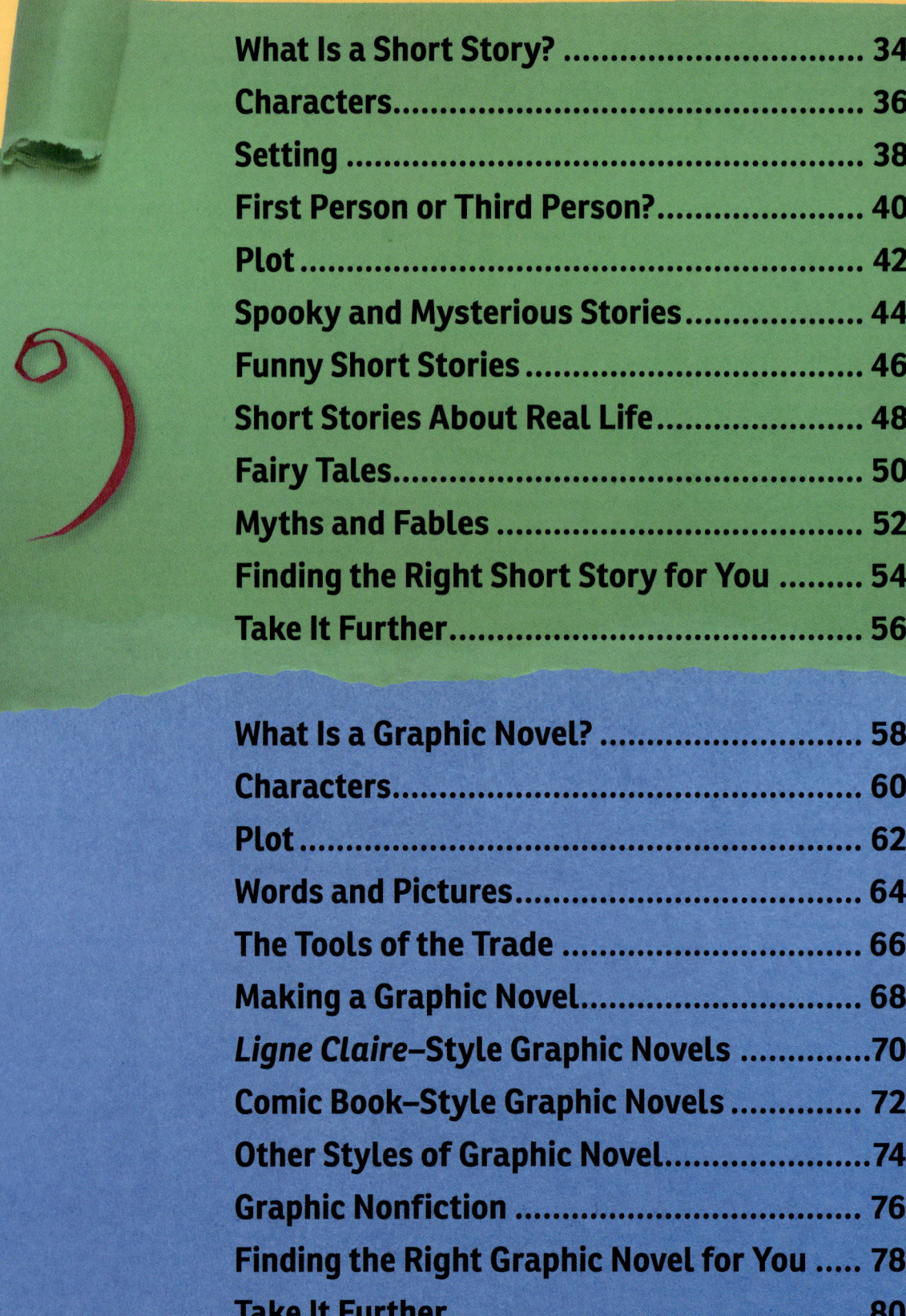

What Is a Short Story? 34
Characters 36
Setting 38
First Person or Third Person? 40
Plot 42
Spooky and Mysterious Stories 44
Funny Short Stories 46
Short Stories About Real Life 48
Fairy Tales 50
Myths and Fables 52
Finding the Right Short Story for You 54
Take It Further 56

What Is a Graphic Novel? 58
Characters 60
Plot 62
Words and Pictures 64
The Tools of the Trade 66
Making a Graphic Novel 68
Ligne Claire–**Style Graphic Novels** 70
Comic Book–Style Graphic Novels 72
Other Styles of Graphic Novel 74
Graphic Nonfiction 76
Finding the Right Graphic Novel for You 78
Take It Further 80

What Is a Poem? 82
What Is Rhythm? 84
What Is a Stanza? 86
Rhyming Patterns 88
Using Sound in Poems 90
What Is Free Verse? 92
Nursery Rhymes 94
Poems That Tell a Story 96
Funny Poems 98
Poems with Patterns 100
Performance Poetry 102
Take It Further 104

Glossary 106
Find Out More 109
Index 111

Some words are shown in bold, **like this**. You can find out what they mean by looking in the glossary.

What Do You Like to Read?

Every day, we all read so many different things. We read instructions in school and messages from friends. You might read magazines. But one of the most enjoyable things to read is a **novel**. When we pick up a novel and start to read, we can be taken away on an amazing adventure or discover another world, full of interesting characters.

Reading a novel can be a great way to relax.

What kind of text do you most enjoy reading?

Maybe you want to read something quick that you can pick up again later, like a comic or a graphic novel. If you like to read a complete story in one reading session, then a short story is perfect. While a novel is like a three-course meal, a short story is like a delicious snack. Or perhaps you enjoy the way poetry can paint a picture in your head and make you see the world differently.

See for yourself

Go to your local library or bookstore and look at the novels on the shelves for your age group. What do the images on the covers tell you about the stories inside? Read the **blurb** on the back cover to see if it grabs your attention and makes you want to read the book.

Want to Try Something New?

Have you ever read any short stories? Perhaps the writers of some of your favorite **novels** have also written short stories. If you look in your library or local bookstore, you might see many collections of short stories on the shelves. If you have never read any stories like this, then give one a try. This book will give you lots of ideas to get you started.

Graphic novels could be a whole new world of reading for you to discover.

You can visit a local bookstore to discover new novels and short stories.

Reading a graphic novel is a very different experience than reading an ordinary novel, but they can both be very exciting. If you like comics, you will probably enjoy graphic novels. If you've never read one, read on to find out more—you might discover something you really like!

See for yourself

Short stories are great for writing competitions because they don't take too long to write and the judges have time to read lots of entries. Search online for prize-winning short stories for children. What do you think makes these stories work?

What Is a Novel?

What makes a novel different than other types of writing? You will often find the following features in a novel:

- The story it tells is **fiction**. Even when a story is based on real events, the author of a novel has researched the real-life experience and created something original.

- Novels have a **narrative** told by a storyteller.

- Novels usually have a certain number of pages and are not too short. Because of their length, novels are usually broken up into chapters or sections.

See for Yourself

We can read novels in different ways. Most novels are published as physical books that we put on our shelves, but many are also published as e-books. People read these on e-readers or on their phones, tablets, or computers. Regardless of which way we read these books, they are still novels.

You may prefer reading novels on an e-reader or from a book.

- Most novels are written in **prose**. This means the language hasn't been organized or made to rhyme like poetry.

- Novels can be written in different **genres**. For example, some novels are adventure stories, while others can be funny or mysterious.

Characters

When you read a good novel, you feel like you are getting to know the main characters. You may even miss them after you finish reading the story! Real and believable characters are important for a story to work well.

Write your own

When you are developing characters for your own stories, start by asking lots of questions about them. What are their names and how old are they? Where do they live and what do they look like? What do they like and dislike? Ask as many questions as you can and get to know your characters as you answer them.

Zeke Meeks is the main character in the *Zeke Meeks vs...* books. Many readers will relate to his love of video games and TV.

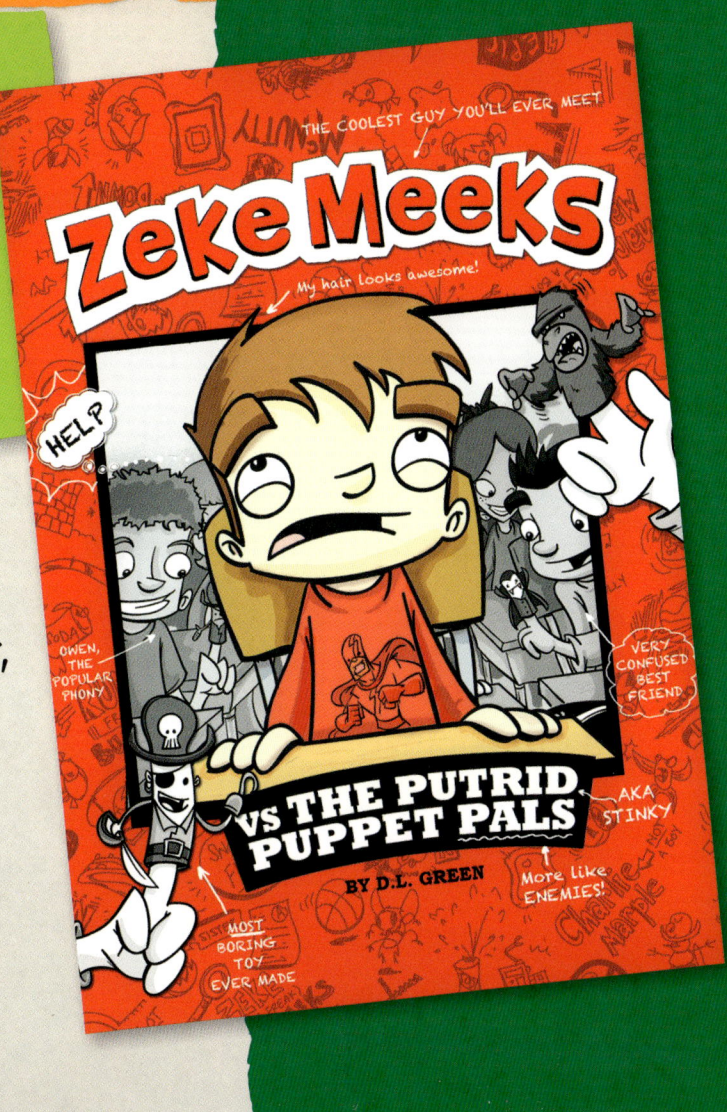

In most novels, there is usually one main character, or **protagonist**, who is the key person we get to know in the story. This person is often trying to reach a goal and has to overcome problems on the way.

Sometimes there might be two or three protagonists, telling the story from different viewpoints. There will also be other types of characters in the story—for example, someone who gets in the way of the protagonist to stop him or her from achieving a goal. Other characters will help or support the main character.

Plot

The **plot** is what happens in a story. Novels are longer than other types of story and can have a more complex plot. Often a novel will have one main plot running through the whole book, with shorter subplots cropping up at different stages of the story. The main plot will usually revolve around what the main character wants. As this character tries to achieve a goal, his or her decisions and activities affect what happens in the plot.

Many writers plan the plots of their stories on cards so they can move things around.

Famous fiction

Jeff Kinney, author of *Diary of a Wimpy Kid*, starts his books by thinking of lots of good jokes. He then sees how he can link up the jokes and find a theme to create a plot for a new story. He writes several different drafts of the story, developing and changing the plot each time.

Jeff Kinney is a cartoonist as well as a writer.

In most good stories, there will often be a moment when the main character is in trouble, and it seems impossible for the character to get what he or she wants. It is usually followed by the character overcoming his or her problems and moving on. Some stories have a surprising twist at the end to keep readers on their toes!

Voice and Tense

The "voice" of a story is important. Some novels are written in the **first person**—for example, "I walked down the path." The main character narrates the story from his or her viewpoint and it seems as if the character is talking directly to us, telling us about his or her thoughts and feelings. In a first-person story, the reader only knows the narrator's viewpoint.

Hearing authors read their own work is very exciting.

In a **third-person** voice, the author stands back from the characters and describes what they think and do—for example, "Joe walked down the path." The writer can tell us about different characters' viewpoints, so we get more information about what is happening.

Are your favorite novels written in the first or third person?

Writers also have to choose which tense to write in. If they write in the **present tense**—"She climbs up the tree"—the story can feel very immediate and exciting. Other stories are written in the **past tense**—"She climbed up the tree."

Write your own

When you have an idea for a story, experiment with the voice and tense before writing. How does your storytelling change if you switch from the third person to the first person? Will your story fit the past tense, or would it be more exciting in the present tense?

Adventure Stories

Lots of people love adventure stories. These novels are popular because the characters are taken away from their everyday lives and often have to overcome danger in order to reach their goal. This makes the stories very exciting!

Adventure stories have been popular for many years, and some classic adventure novels are still read a lot today, such as *The Silver Sword* and *Treasure Island.*

Treasure Island is a thrilling adventure story, full of pirates and chests of gold.

Famous fiction

Willard Price wrote exciting adventure stories for children, such as *Volcano Adventure* and *Arctic Adventure*. In these stories, two teenagers named Hal and Roger travel the world, saving animals and surviving danger! In 2011, *Leopard Adventure*, the first of a new series of stories about Hal's son and Roger's daughter, was published. Anthony McGowan is writing the new books, which should appeal to readers who loved the first series.

Anthony McGowan is a prize-winning author of books for children and young adults.

A good adventure story should:

- be completely gripping so that the reader doesn't want to stop turning the pages

- be full of surprises so that the reader doesn't know what will happen next

- include strong, brave heroes who are not afraid to take risks, and wonderfully wicked villains who will stop at nothing to get what they want

- completely take the reader away from reality.

Funny Novels

Funny novels are very popular. Most people enjoy laughing and sharing the jokes in a book with their friends. Making readers laugh out loud is very hard for writers to achieve and takes a lot of skill and practice. The funniest writers read a lot of other humorous books and watch funny movies and television shows.

Cressida Cowell has sold millions of copies of her entertaining stories.

Famous fiction

The *Mr. Gum* books by Andy Stanton are famously funny, but they don't follow all the rules we expect with a novel. The plots of the stories are often completely crazy, and Andy plays around with language in original and unexpected ways. However, he still includes characters the reader cares about as well as horrible villains who readers love to hate.

Andy's author events are as funny as his books!

The funniest novels have the following features:

- They are original. Writers won't make their readers laugh if they've heard all the jokes and twists before.

- They play around with words in surprising ways. When writers play with the different possible meanings of a word, it is called a **pun**.

- Most funny stories still need to have a strong **plot** that makes sense and believable characters.

Fantasy Novels

If you want to escape from ordinary life for a while, then a fantasy novel is perfect. Fantasy stories take the reader to new worlds that can be filled with magical creatures and powerful heroes and villains. *Harry Potter, The Hobbit, The Worst Witch*, and the *Artemis Fowl* novels are all well-known fantasy books.

Famous fiction

J. K. Rowling's *Harry Potter* books are among the best-known children's fantasy novels in the world. Harry is a young wizard who goes to Hogwarts School of Witchcraft and Wizardry and gets involved in exciting and dangerous adventures. Around 450 million copies of the seven books in the series have been sold, and they have been translated into 67 languages.

J. K. Rowling is one of the most famous authors in the world.

In many fantasy novels, animals have magical powers.

The best fantasy novels often:

- take place in elaborate and magical settings, in completely imaginary worlds.

- involve talking animals and **mythical** creatures. Such characters can have totally different powers and skills than ordinary human characters.

- involve lots of magic. Look out for wizards, witches, fairies, goblins, and many other fantastic magical beings.

- have a gripping **plot**, with the brave heroes or heroines fighting against evil.

Science Fiction

Science fiction is similar to fantasy in many ways. Both types of novel imagine worlds that don't exist, but science fiction uses science as a starting point. Events in a science fiction novel may be possible at some point in the future, while fantasy worlds will never exist. Some science fiction novels are based on popular science fiction movies, such as *Star Wars*, or television series, such as *Doctor Who*.

Science fiction stories often take place on other planets.

Famous fiction

Stephen Hawking is a famous scientist who is well known for his discoveries. He has also written three children's books with his daughter, Lucy Hawking. In the books, a character named George goes on adventures across the universe, exploring black holes, investigating alien life, and fighting evil scientists.

Stephen Hawking has often written about the science of the universe.

Science fiction novels usually have the following things in common:

- The writer gives a scientific explanation for what happens in the **plot**.

- The story can take the reader away from his or her own life and world.

- The stories are often set far in the future.

- The novels often include amazing inventions and discoveries and may involve traveling through time.

Mystery Stories

Many people enjoy mystery or detective stories. In these novels, the main characters have a problem to solve. This could be a mystery that needs unraveling or a crime that needs to be solved. People enjoy reading mystery stories because they like solving the puzzle of what will happen.

Famous fiction

Some classic mystery stories include Gertrude Chandler Warner's *Boxcar Children* series, Donald J. Sobol's *Encyclopedia Brown* series, and *The Hardy Boys* and *Nancy Drew* stories. More recently, many readers have also enjoyed Lauren Child's *Ruby Redfort* books and John Grisham's series *Theodore Boone*, about a mystery-solving teen.

John Grisham is a best-selling author of exciting thrillers for children and adults.

When you read a mystery story, you can look for clues, just like the characters!

A good mystery story includes the following things:

- It has unexpected twists that take the reader by surprise. There might also be **red herrings**, which mislead the readers and make them think something else has happened before the truth is revealed.

- The writer slowly reveals clues that the readers can use to figure out for themselves what is happening in the story.

- The stories tend to have very tight **plots**, with the details in every twist and turn making complete sense.

Realistic Stories

Some readers like stories that are set in the real world. These stories explore what life is like for many people and share true experiences with readers, rather than taking them away to a made-up world.

Realistic novels have the following features:

- The stories have recognizable settings and characters. The places and people may be in a very different part of the world, but they are based in reality.

- Writers often put their characters in difficult or sad situations. The **plot** often involves the main **protagonists** struggling to overcome these difficulties.

Laura Ingalls Wilder wrote stories based on her own experiences of growing up in the Midwest.

- The reader really cares about and **empathizes** with the characters in a realistic novel.

- Many realistic novels are set in a different time in history. They might be based on real people and events, or they can be entirely fictional.

- The writer of a realistic novel needs to be careful to include many accurate details, to make the world of the story seem real.

Michael Morpurgo has written several books set during World War I and World War II.

Write your own

If you want to write a story, it might be easiest to write something realistic. Think about interesting experiences you have had in your life and the people you know. You could tell a story that will be very different than other people's lives.

Finding the Right Novel for You

If you already enjoy reading novels, perhaps you could try a **genre** you haven't read before. For example, if you've always read realistic stories, you could try some fantasy or science fiction. Or if you normally stick to books that make you laugh, you could try something different, like a mystery story.

Explore different genres and discover new favorites.

Maybe you are someone who doesn't normally enjoy reading novels. It might be that you haven't found the right book for you yet. Think about what you enjoy. If you like reading comics and watching funny shows on television, you might enjoy funny books. If you like nonfiction and finding out facts, you will probably prefer a realistic novel. You could also talk to a librarian or bookseller or ask your friends about the books they enjoy.

See for yourself

You could start a book club at your school. Get together with a group of readers and take turns recommending books. You could lend books to members of your group or swap stories after you have finished reading them. Encourage one another to try something new!

Take It Further...

Do you want to write your own novel? Here are some ways to get started:

1. Always carry a notebook and pen so you can jot down ideas when they pop into your head.

2. Try to read as many books in as many different **genres** as you can.

3. Think carefully about the setting of your story. How can you describe it so the reader really feels what the world in your story is like?

4. Think carefully about your main **protagonist** and all the other characters in your story. Ask yourself lots of questions about each character so you are very clear what they are like.

5. Figure out the **plot** of your story. Think about the problems your main character is going to face and how he or she will overcome them. Who or what will get in his or her way? Can you think of a twist at the end of the story?

6. Keep editing your story until you are happy with it.

Ideas to get you started

Your main character's dog has disappeared. The newspaper is reporting that pets are vanishing all over town. Can your hero solve the mystery of the missing animals?

Your spacecraft has landed on a faraway planet. You are stepping out onto the planet's surface, looking for signs of life. Suddenly, you hear a loud explosion...

Your main character's best friend in school has started bullying other kids. What has made the friend change his or her behavior? Will your main character be able to stop the bully, or will he or she be bullied, too?

What Is a Short Story?

A short story is different than a **novel** or poem. It usually has the following features:

- A short story is **fiction**—the writer is telling the reader a story that he or she created, even if the writer got the idea from something that really happened.

- A short story is written in **prose**. This means it is not written in verse, like lots of poetry.

- Short stories are much shorter than novels. Often you can read a short story in one sitting, while a novel might take much longer. Short stories are not divided into chapters, but they often focus on one or two moments or events.

See For Yourself

Find a short story and look for the following:
- How many characters are there?
- Where does the story take place?
- How much time passes during the story?

Most short stories include just a few characters in one place for only a short length of time.

- A short story usually only has a few characters. The writer really focuses on these people and what is happening to them.

- Lots of short stories have a surprise twist at the end.

- Short stories often appear in a collection with other stories. Sometimes they are published in magazines.

Do you read any magazines that have short stories in them?

Characters

While a **novel** can have many characters with very different experiences and outlooks, a short story focuses in more closely on one or only a few characters. During the story, we learn about this character's personality and his or her actions in a short space of time, unlike in a novel, where we can read about a character over many years. This means that when we read about a character in a short story, we are really zooming in on a part of his or her life and personality and exploring it in depth.

You get to know a character very quickly in a short story.

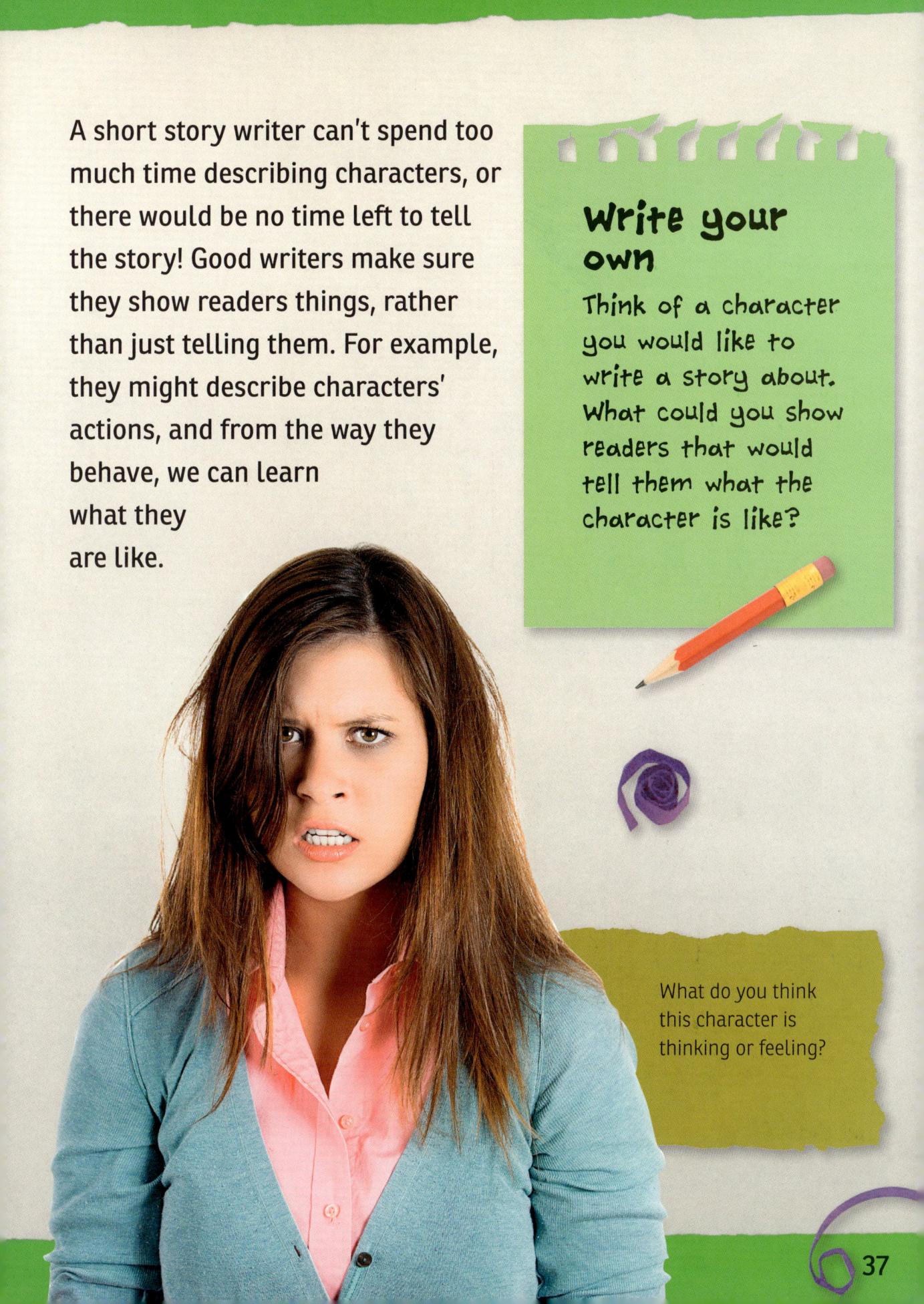

A short story writer can't spend too much time describing characters, or there would be no time left to tell the story! Good writers make sure they show readers things, rather than just telling them. For example, they might describe characters' actions, and from the way they behave, we can learn what they are like.

Write your own

Think of a character you would like to write a story about. What could you show readers that would tell them what the character is like?

What do you think this character is thinking or feeling?

37

Setting

When starting to create a new short story, a writer thinks about the **setting**. This is where the events of the story take place, and it could be a house, a city street, or inside a spaceship. The setting also includes the time, season, and weather.

In a short story, the setting is important because it sets the mood. A strong setting builds atmosphere and helps to keep the reader hooked.

What sort of story might have a setting like this?

How would you describe the sights, sounds, and smells of a setting like this?

Short story writers often use all of the senses to describe a setting. They think about what it looks like, the sounds and smells that the characters are experiencing, and even how things taste and feel. Using all of the senses makes sure the reader can imagine the setting very clearly. This means the writer can move forward with telling the story.

Write your own

Close your eyes and think about the place where you want to set your story. What can you see and hear? Are there any smells around you? Are you hot or cold? Ask yourself lots of questions before you start to write.

First Person or Third Person?

Short story writers have to decide whether to write in the **first person** or **third person**. Stories in the first person are told from the main character's perspective. This person narrates the story and talks about "I"—for example, "I waded across the flooded street." The main advantage of writing in the first person is that readers feel close to the narrator. This means they can really get "under the skin" of the main character and get to know him or her well.

Sometimes writers try the first and third person before deciding which one to use in their story.

Charles Dickens also wrote novels in the first and third person.

Famous fiction

Charles Dickens (1812–1870) was a writer who wrote both long **novels** and short stories. *The Long Voyage* is a short story told in the first person by a character who loves to read about exciting adventures, but has never been anywhere himself. Because this story is short, using the first person allows Dickens to show us a lot about this main character and how he feels.

Other stories are written in the third person. This is when the writer steps back and describes what is happening to the characters from the writer's or narrator's viewpoint—for example, "Jenny waded across the flooded street." With the third person, the writer is able to tell us about what more than one character is thinking.

Plot

The **plot** is what happens in the story. When writers plan their stories, they often begin with the plot. They figure out what events will take place and in what order. It's important that the plot makes complete sense and has no loose ends.

The plot of a story must be original to keep the reader interested.

A story with a gripping plot will be hard to put down.

Usually what the main character in the story wants affects what happens in the plot. In a short story, there will only be one or a few events, with a problem that the main character will have to overcome. There is often a surprise or twist at the end that the reader didn't see coming! In a short story, everything that happens in the plot needs to be included for a reason. There is no room for extra details that are not important or for **subplots**.

Write your own

When you are creating a plot for a short story, start with a main character. What does he or she want more than anything? What could be standing in the way of this? How will the character deal with it? Then, think of an ending that will surprise your readers.

Spooky and Mysterious Stories

Many well-known short stories are spooky or mysterious. Some of the most famous ghost stories and detective stories are short stories. A British writer named Arthur Conan Doyle wrote short stories about the detective Sherlock Holmes. In each tale, Holmes solves a crime or mystery with his sidekick, Dr. Watson, often facing danger along the way. The American writer Edgar Allan Poe was well known for his scary short stories. Many of these are full of haunted houses and unexplained deaths.

Sherlock Holmes is one of the most famous fictional detectives in the world.

Famous fiction

You may have read some of Roald Dahl's children's books, such as *Charlie and the Chocolate Factory* and *Matilda*. He also wrote very scary short stories for adults! Many of these have a dark sense of humor, and they often have shocking **plot** twists. Some of Dahl's short stories were filmed for television.

Many of Roald Dahl's stories have dark and shocking characters.

Many of these **narratives** are told as short stories because this allowed the writer to keep up the tension. It would be much harder to keep the reader in **suspense** in a longer **novel**. Also, lots of these stories were first published in magazines, so they had to be quite short!

Funny Short Stories

A short story is a good way to tell a funny tale, because the writer can focus on a central joke and build up a hilarious situation around a single moment or short sequence of events. The twist at the end of a short story can work in the same way as the **punch line** of a joke.

Mark Twain was well known for his sense of humor.

Famous fiction

Author Francesca Simon created the children's book character Horrid Henry. He appears in books made up of several short stories. Each one takes Henry through a funny situation. Even though he is quite horrible, the reader wants Henry to succeed—but he usually gets his comeuppance in the end.

Horrid Henry is a favorite funny children's book character.

Mark Twain was an American writer who wrote witty short stories as well as longer **novels**, such as *The Adventures of Tom Sawyer*. His short stories were published in newspapers and magazines. He also read them out loud to audiences around the United States. The short story suited these events perfectly because he could read a complete story to the people listening. Many of Twain's funny short stories were based on **observations** he had made in his own life about how people could be vain or foolish or how they misunderstood each other.

Short Stories About Real Life

A lot of short story writers choose to describe real-life situations in their stories. They show us realistic moments in their characters' lives that might pass very quickly. Despite being only a small glimpse, the events in a good short story will stay in the reader's mind for a long time. When short stories are about real-life situations, the **settings** and characters are often very vivid and can feel real to the reader.

Atinuke's stories show us what real life is like in many parts of Africa.

Famous fiction

The Canadian writer Alice Munro is one of the world's most famous authors of short stories. She writes about people living in small towns who are facing problems in their apparently ordinary lives. The situations she describes often leave readers thinking about what they have just witnessed.

Alice Munro has won many prizes for her writing.

There are many short stories for children about people's "ordinary" lives. These include the *Anna Hibiscus* books written by Atinuke. These stories, about a girl growing up with her **extended family** in a busy African city, pick up on problems and experiences that all children are familiar with.

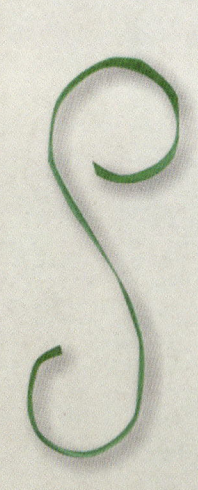

Fairy Tales

Some of the first stories we ever hear are short stories. Fairy tales have been told and retold to children for centuries and are perfect examples of short stories.

Famous fiction

Some of Hans Christian Andersen's most famous stories are *The Princess and the Pea*, *The Little Mermaid*, and *The Emperor's New Clothes*. His stories often show readers that appearances are only skin-deep and that it's not right to judge people based on how they look or how wealthy they are.

Hans Christian Andersen (1805–1875) was a Danish writer who created many fairy tales.

The Brothers Grimm began writing down the folk tales they heard when they were growing up in Germany. Jacob (1785–1863) and Wilhelm (1786–1859) Grimm collected fairy stories and folk tales, such as *Cinderella*, *Hansel and Gretel*, and *Snow White*. They wanted to discover and share the stories enjoyed by ordinary German people. Because these stories were originally told from memory, there were often different versions of them. The Brothers Grimm helped to create the version of each story that we know today.

The Brothers Grimm told one version of the *Little Red Riding Hood* story.

Myths and Fables

The oldest short stories ever told or written down were probably **myths** and **fables**. Myths are very old, traditional stories that are often about ancient gods and heroes. For example, Greek myths are the stories and ideas of the ancient Greeks.

The ancient Greeks believed the stories told in their myths to be true. They described powerful gods and goddesses and the actions of brave heroes and heroines. The most famous myths include the story of Icarus, who flew too close to the Sun, and King Midas, who wished that everything he touched would turn to gold.

Icarus's wings were made out of feathers and wax by his father, Daedalus.

Fables are stories with a moral or lesson at the end. These stories are often short and involve just a few characters, usually animals. Some well-known fables are *The Hare and the Tortoise* and *The Lion and the Mouse*.

Write your own

Try writing your own fable. It's easiest to start with a moral, such as "appearances can be deceiving," "don't trust people who flatter you," or "the biggest isn't always the best." Try to build a story that shows this moral, with animals as your characters.

Finding the Right Short Story for You

You have to hunt for short stories a bit more than other types of story. Often they are put in collections with other stories by different authors. This means you might discover new writers as you make your way through a collection. These books are also great to jump in and out of, because you don't have to follow a long **narrative** over time, as you do with a **novel**.

Discover new authors as you explore short story collections.

There are many short stories to enjoy when you know where to look for them.

It's a good idea to ask a librarian or bookseller for advice on finding different collections of short stories. If you want funny or spooky stories, they might be able to suggest suitable collections. Or, if you like an author's style, they might be able to suggest a collection of that author's short stories.

Another place to find short stories is in magazines and comics. You could read them aloud with your friends and family and then talk about them afterward.

See for yourself

Visit a web site that sells books and search for "short stories for children." Take a look at the collections that come up and see if you are interested in any of them. If you are, you could borrow the book from your library or even buy a copy.

Take It Further...

If you want to write a short story:

1. Always carry a notebook and pen so you can jot down ideas. This could be when you're on the school bus or walking around the grocery store!

2. Think carefully about the main character in your story. What does he or she want more than anything? How can you describe your character so that the reader knows as much as possible about his or her personality?

3. Spend time thinking about where and when your story is taking place. Close your eyes and ask yourself questions about the **setting**. Try to describe it so it appeals to all of the reader's senses.

4. Keep your **plot** simple and clear, with no unexplained events that are not important to the story. And try to come up with a surprise twist at the end!

Ideas to get you started

Your character got into trouble at school. He or she goes home and finds his or her mother on the phone with the principal. What does your character do?

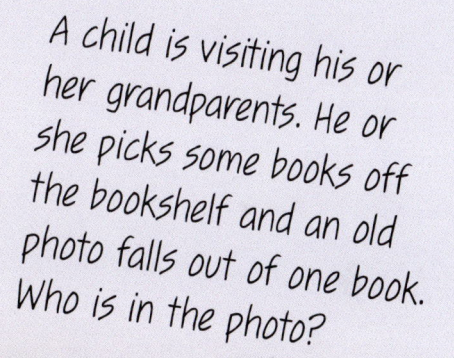

A child is visiting his or her grandparents. He or she picks some books off the bookshelf and an old photo falls out of one book. Who is in the photo?

Your main character is hiking through the woods on a school trip. But he or she is separated from the group and gets lost. It's starting to get dark…

What Is a Graphic Novel?

A graphic novel is different than comics and other books in several ways. The main feature of a graphic novel is that it is a complete story made up of words and pictures, and it is drawn in a comic strip **format**. Stories in comics are often published in weekly **episodes**—so you may have to wait to find out what happens next! Sometimes lots of comic strip episodes are put together to make a graphic novel.

Famous fiction

The writer Neil Gaiman has written stories for comic books, such as *The Sandman*. Originally, the stories were published in monthly episodes by DC Comics. They were so popular that the episodes were later collected together and published as a complete graphic novel.

Neil Gaiman has written many different types of book, including graphic novels.

In graphic novels, the characters' speech and thoughts are set in speech bubbles. This means you won't see quotation marks, like you would in an ordinary novel.

A graphic novel can be fiction or nonfiction. Many graphic novels tell fantastical stories. Others are **biographies** or tell the reader about real historical events.

We barely escaped the doomed ship by clinging to a raft of planks and hollow barrels.

We're ashore!

Is everyone all right?

I'm thirsty, Father.

Here, sip it slowly.

Are we on an island, Father?

Good question. It might be a **peninsula**.

Father! Help!!

Quotation marks aren't used in a graphic novel.

Characters

The characters are the people we get to know as a story unfolds. In ordinary novels, writers need to describe their characters so we know what they look like and how they behave. In a graphic novel, the writer doesn't need to describe the characters because the pictures show all their **features**. In fact, a graphic novel can tell us a lot more about characters in just a glance.

BATMAN © DC Comics

Famous fiction

The character Batman was created in 1939 by illustrator Bob Kane. Stories about Batman were published by DC Comics and became very popular. Today, Batman is also a well-known character in movies and on television.

In a graphic novel, there is usually a main hero, or **protagonist**. These characters normally want something and have to overcome challenges to achieve their goals. There are also other characters who help the heroes—and villains who try to stop them. It's important that all the characters look different from each other because the reader won't be told who is speaking, as in an ordinary novel. We have to recognize who is speaking by looking at each illustration.

Many of the best stories are about a battle between good and evil.

Plot

Like all stories, a graphic novel needs to have a gripping **plot** to keep the reader turning the page. Lots of stories start with an exciting opening, followed by a series of events where the hero is trying to get what he or she wants. There is often a twist at the end to surprise the reader!

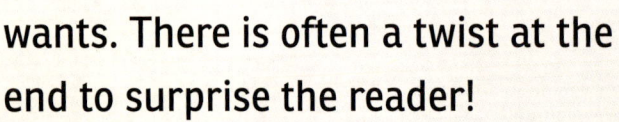

Many writers spend a lot of time planning the plots of their stories.

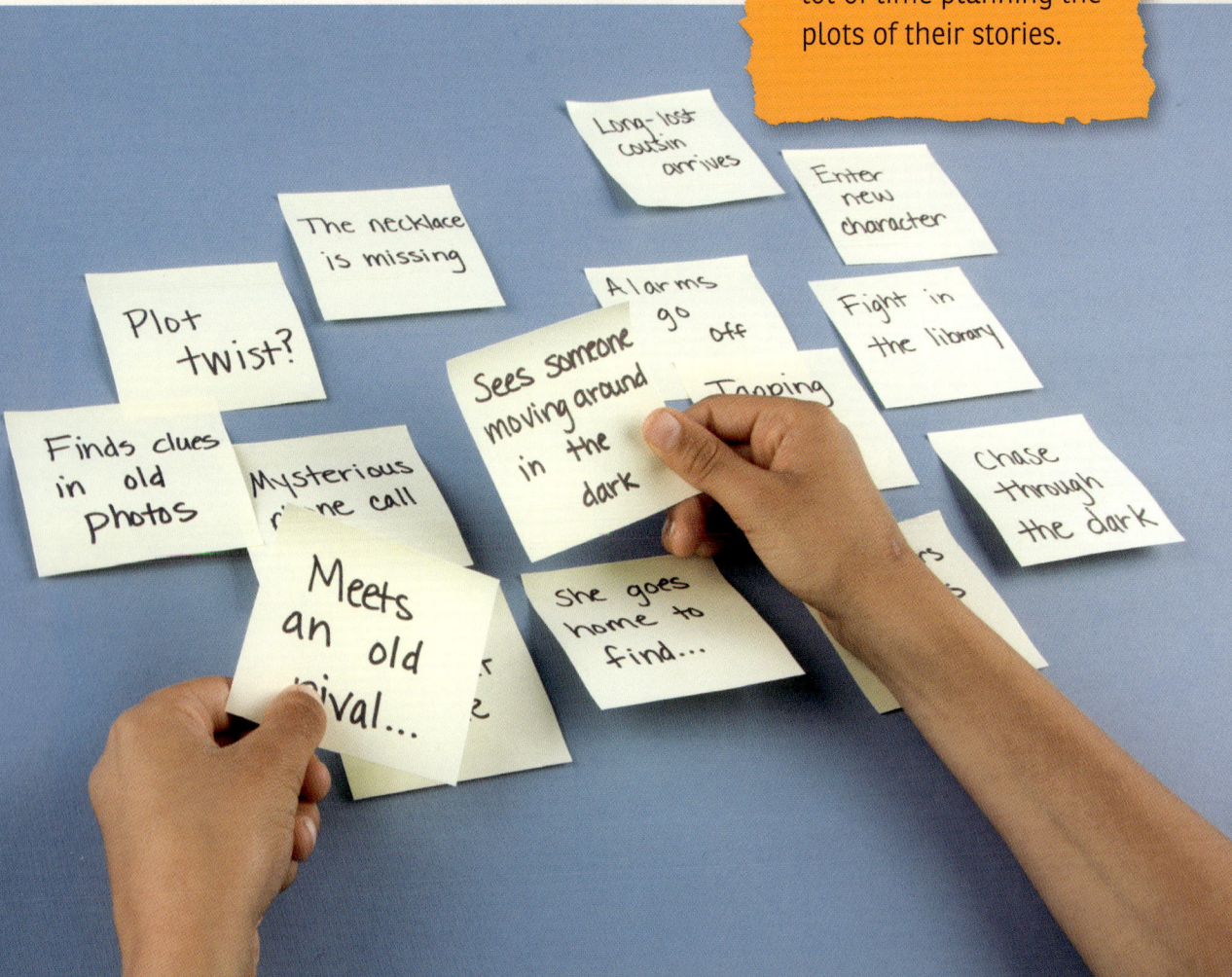

Famous fiction

Graphic novels that were first published as stories in comics would have come in weekly or monthly installments. Each **episode** would usually end on a cliffhanger moment to make the reader want to buy the next edition. When these installments are put together to make a graphic novel, it can make an exciting plot that is full of tense moments.

The plot in a graphic novel is often shorter than in an ordinary novel. This is because the images that tell so much of the story take up a lot of space and show detailed scenes on every spread.

Pictures can tell much of the plot without any words at all.

Words and Pictures

With some graphic novels, the same person comes up with the story and draws the pictures. With others, one person writes the words and another person illustrates them. The writer might work with the illustrator as he or she develops the story, so they both have ideas about the finished text. The pictures can show all sorts of information that there wouldn't be space to describe in words. An illustration can also have a much greater impact than a lot of text.

Famous fiction

Dave Gibbons is a British artist who is well known for his illustrations of superheroes in comic books and graphic novels. He has created the images for stories about Doctor Who, Green Lantern, and Watchmen. The *Watchmen* graphic novel, illustrated by Gibbons, is one of the best-selling graphic novels.

Neil Gaiman has worked closely with the illustrator Dave McKean on several of his books.

Another benefit of reading graphic novels is that if you sometimes come across words that you haven't seen before, the pictures might help you to understand what they mean without having to reach for a dictionary!

The Tools of the Trade

Traditionally, people who write and illustrate graphic novels start with a pencil and paper. They produce many sketches as they develop each character and give them a distinctive look. Today, some graphic novel creators draw straight onto a computer. Others sketch out their pictures in pencil first and then scan them in. Special computer software can make the illustrations sharper and more finished, and then the illustrator can add color.

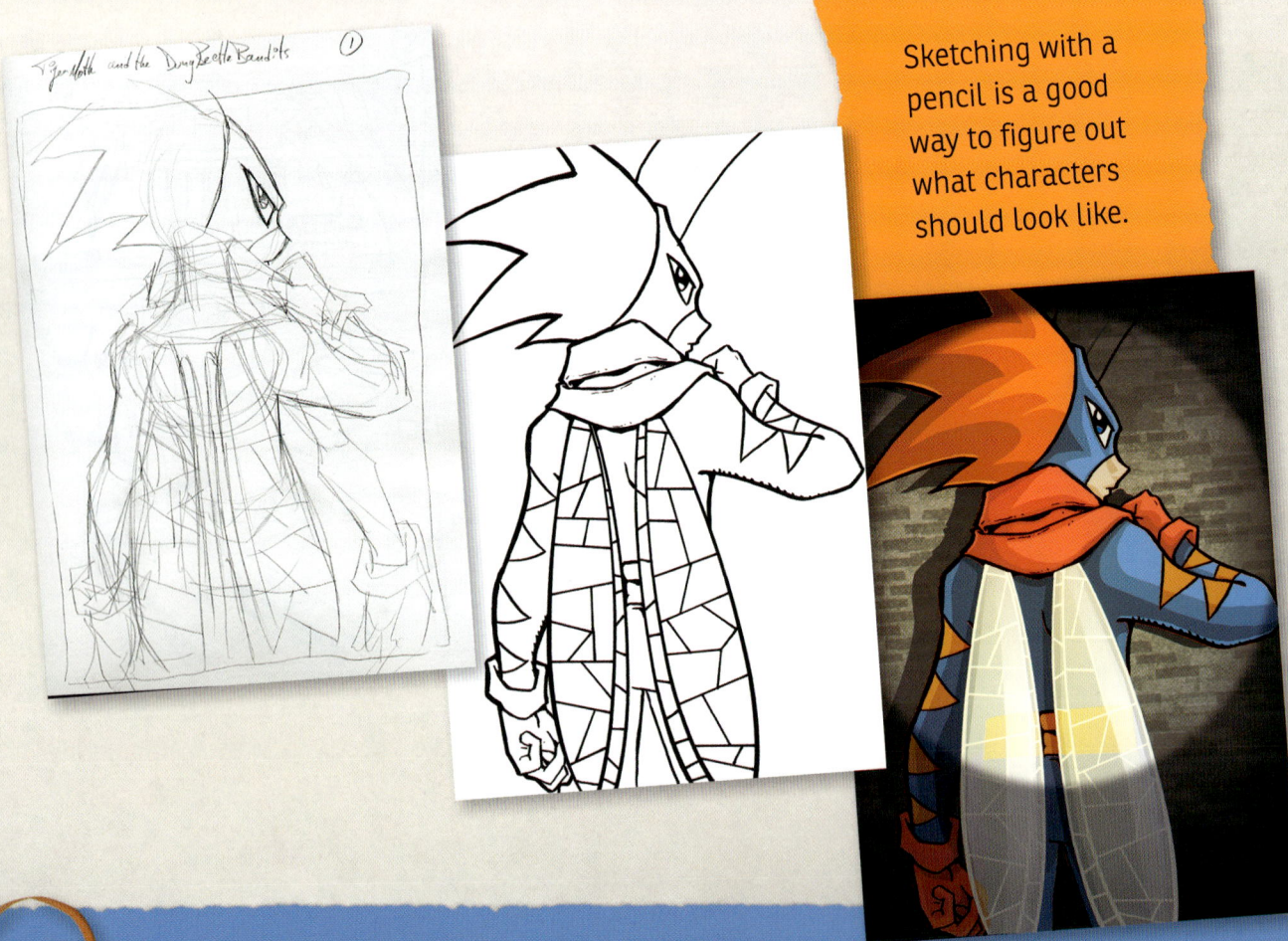

Sketching with a pencil is a good way to figure out what characters should look like.

Illustrators need to have all the right tools before they can start work.

The most important tools a graphic novel writer and artist needs are:

- plenty of paper
- a ruler
- a pencil
- an eraser
- a thin black drawing pen
- colored pencils, pens, or inks.

Write your own

Make sure you start with a very soft pencil. You will need to make your drawings very light so that you can easily erase the pencil marks after you have gone over them in pen.

Making a Graphic Novel

Graphic novel writers start by planning out their story. They need a strong **plot** and different characters. The illustrator makes lots of sketches of each character to show what clothes and belongings they have.

Next, they make rough plans to show which part of the story will be told on each page. This is called a **storyboard**. They mark out boxes that show each stage in the story sequence and make rough sketches of what will happen in each box.

The storyboard starts as a rough sketch so it's easy to make changes.

Write your own

The last picture on each right-hand page of a graphic novel is important. It's good to show an exciting moment here, so the reader can't wait to turn the page and see what happens next. There might be a question or a joke there, so the reader has to turn the page to find the answer or **punch line!**

Then, the illustrator gradually adds more and more detail.

When they have drawn a storyboard, they make the pictures more detailed using a soft pencil before going over them in pen. Then, they add color. It's important to leave enough room in each panel for all the words in speech bubbles and boxes!

Ligne Claire–Style Graphic Novels

The illustrations in graphic novels can be drawn in different styles. The artwork style used in the *Tintin* books by the Belgian writer and illustrator Hergé is called **ligne claire**. This means "clear line" in French. It has this name because all the strong, black outlines in the drawing are the same thickness. The illustrator doesn't use different widths of line to show parts of the picture that are near, or far, or in shadow. Bold blocks of color are used rather than complicated **shading**. This style has a very clear and simple effect.

Hergé's *Tintin* books have been translated into many different languages.

Hergé produced *Tintin* books until he died in 1983.

Hergé was one of the first illustrators to use this drawing style in the 1940s. During World War II, it was impossible to import comic books from the United States, so European artists developed their own, quite different style.

Famous fiction

Garen Ewing wrote and illustrated the *Rainbow Orchid* books. These graphic novels are about the adventures of a young historical researcher named Julius Chancer. Ewing started creating these stories in the 1990s, but the *ligne claire* style perfectly suits his stories, which are set in the 1920s.

Comic Book–Style Graphic Novels

American comic books started to become popular in the late 1930s and during the 1940s. The stories were often about superheroes, such as Spider-Man, Superman, and Batman. The illustrations usually include lots of detail, and the artists draw lines of different thickness to create depth and shade. They often use a technique called **cross-hatching** and sometimes use blocks of black ink to create a bold, striking effect.

Cross-hatching is where lines are layered in different directions to add **shading**.

This comic book style is used in many graphic novels today. Illustrators show some scenes very close up or from unusual angles, and they can show a lot of movement. The characters often have very exaggerated **features**—for example, huge muscles and chiseled faces.

SCREECH!!

Metal tore as the iceberg ripped through the hull. Instantly, thousands of gallons of water poured into the lower areas of the ship.

Famous fiction

Writer Jerry Siegel and illustrator Joe Shuster were still in school when they created the character of Superman in the 1930s. A few years later, it was bought by the company now known as DC Comics. Since then, Superman has starred in many graphic novels as well as movies, cartoons, comic books, and television series.

Sometimes text is used as part of the artwork to create sound effects.

Other Styles of Graphic Novel

Many other drawing styles are used in graphic novels. Some illustrators use a very cartoony style—for example, in the *Asterix* books by René Goscinny and Albert Uderzo. The characters started out as a serial comic strip in a French magazine, but they went on to star in many hilarious graphic novels, cartoons, and movies.

The *Asterix* graphic novels have been translated into many languages.

The **manga** style of artwork developed in Japan and has become very popular across the world. Manga stories tend to follow themes, such as romance, adventure, magic, or school life. A manga-style graphic novel can be hundreds of pages long.

Manga characters often have large eyes and unusually styled hair.

Famous fiction

Many graphic novels for children are produced by children's picture book illustrators. Raymond Briggs writes and illustrates stories such as *The Snowman* and *Fungus the Bogeyman*. These are sold as picture books, but they are really graphic novels. Shaun Tan's *The Arrival* could be described as a wordless graphic novel. Illustrators such as Sarah McIntyre illustrate picture books and children's novels in addition to creating comics and graphic novels.

Graphic Nonfiction

Graphic novels are not just a great way to tell a fictional story. The unique combination of words and images is also a great way to describe all sorts of nonfiction subjects. Many graphic novelists have told their own **autobiography** or another person's **biography** using this type of text.

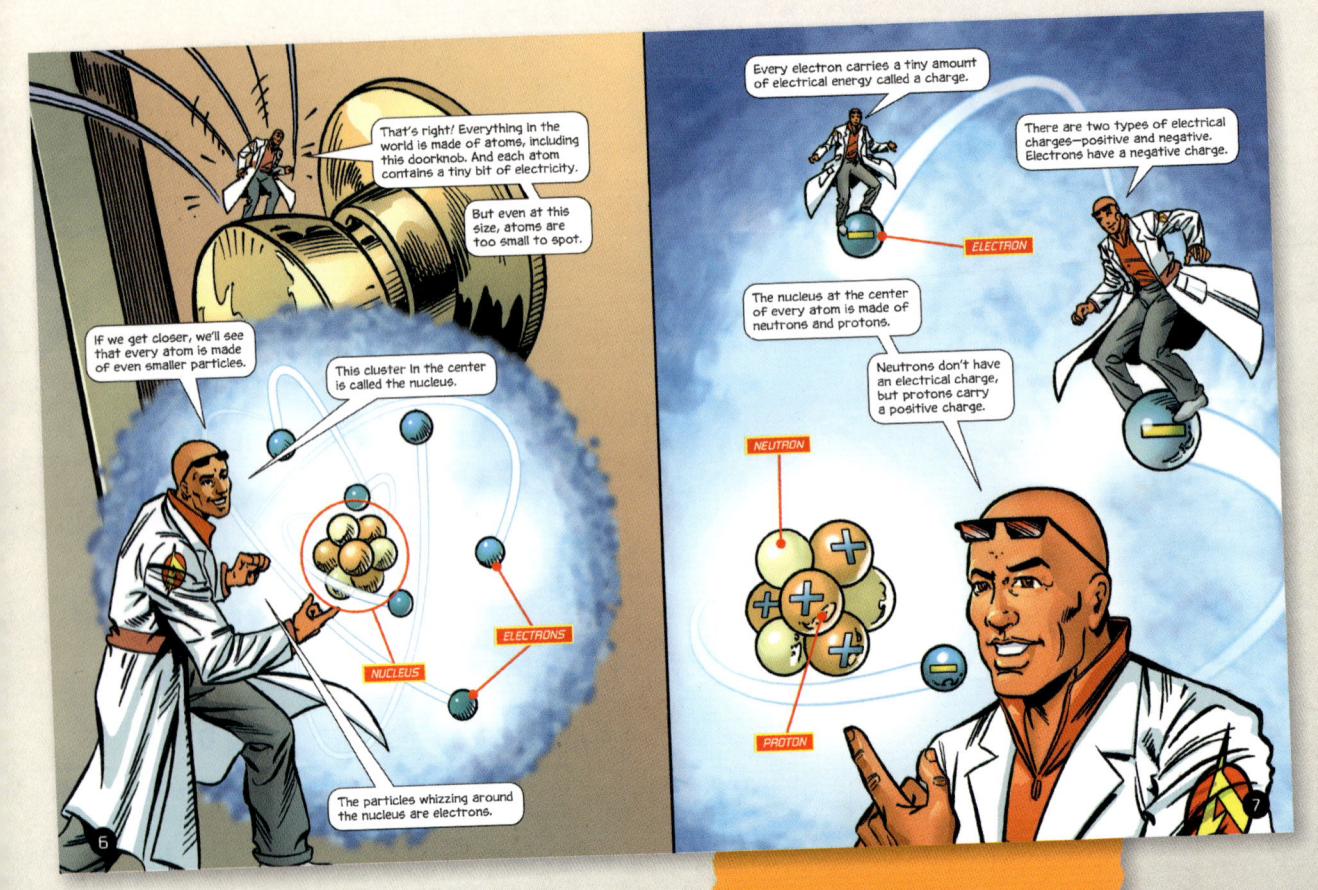

Graphic nonfiction can explain complex ideas in a clear, visual way.

76

Subjects such as science and history can also be described and explained using a graphic novel **format**. The illustrations can help to explain difficult ideas in a clearer way. Historical events can be brought to life, with clothing and **artifacts** shown in detail.

Graphic nonfiction can make stories from history interesting and exciting.

Write your own

Why not try writing an extract from your own autobiography in a graphic novel style? Choose an event from your life that you want to share. Who was involved? Draw the different "characters." Then, work up a rough **storyboard** to show what happened.

Finding the Right Graphic Novel for You

If you've never read a graphic novel, are you wondering where to start? If you read a comic, maybe some of the writers and illustrators have also produced graphic novels. For example, Jamie Smart has written and illustrated comic strips in *The Phoenix* comic and has also published the graphic novel *Fish-Head Steve*.

You may find graphic novels about characters you have seen in movies or on television.

You could look at the comic's web site or look up the writers' and illustrators' own web sites to find out what else they have created.

You could also ask your librarian, local bookseller, or teacher to recommend a graphic novel. If you normally like adventure books, prefer funny books, or always read mystery stories, then there will probably be a graphic novel that is right for you. If you've read a good graphic novel, lend it to a friend and see what he or she thinks. Can your friends suggest any graphic novels that they have enjoyed reading?

If your friends read graphic novels, ask them for some recommendations.

See for yourself

Visit one of the web sites at the back of this book and search for graphic novels for children your age. Has anyone written a review of the books? Why not borrow one from your library and see what it's like?

Take It Further...

Do you want to create your own graphic novel? Here are some ways to get started:

1. Read as many comics and graphic novels as you can. Think about how the story is told using the pictures as much as the words.

2. Look at different artwork styles and decide if you want to try to draw in one of those styles. Try copying the way some of the characters have been drawn.

3. Come up with a good story. Make sure you include some good twists!

4. Draw sketches of all the characters in your story. Do they all look and behave differently enough to prevent the reader from getting confused?

5. Sketch out a **storyboard**, making sure you show all the important stages of the story. You could make some panels extra big if you want these sections to stand out.

6. Draw each panel in more detail with a soft pencil, including your speech bubbles and text boxes. Then, go over the top with a black drawing pen. After you have erased the pencil lines, add color and write the speech bubbles and other words.

Ideas to get you started

An evil genius is threatening to drain all the water out of the city and force the people who live there to work as his slaves. Only one hero can save the day...

A schoolgirl has magical powers that she uses to try to help people. But sometimes her good ideas backfire!

Thieves have stolen a priceless carving from the museum. Nobody knows where the thieves are, but they have left some important clues behind. Who can solve the clues and track the carving down?

What Is a Poem?

A poem is a piece of text that has been written in a particular way. You'll notice the following things about poems:

- They are written so that the sound and the meaning of the words make the reader feel and think in certain ways. A poem often appeals to all of the reader's or listener's senses.

- Poems can be long or short. They can tell a story or just create a mood.

- A poem uses **rhythm** in special ways to have an effect on the reader. For example, a gentle, flowing rhythm might make the reader feel calm and relaxed.

- Some poems involve **rhyme**. This means that words at the end of some lines have similar sounds. Other poems don't rhyme.

- Some poems have very fixed structures. These can involve a set number of lines or the rhythm of each line. Other poems have no rules at all!

Popular poems

William Shakespeare is one of the most famous writers in the English language. Shakespeare is best known for his plays, but he also wrote poems. The most famous of these are the 154 **sonnets** he wrote about subjects like love and death. Sonnets have a special structure, and most have 14 lines.

Poetry can range from works by Shakespeare to the **lyrics** of a song.

What Is Rhythm?

Rhythm is very important in poetry. The rhythm makes a poem sound very different than **prose**, which is the type of language used in most novels and short stories. When you hear a poem or listen to a song, there is a pattern of sound that is repeated. This regular beat is called the rhythm.

The rhythm can make the poem flow well, or it can have a jerky, awkward effect that can make readers feel the way the poet wants them to. Some poems have a rhythm that sounds like the subject of the poem—for example, a poem about a train might sound like an engine clattering along a track.

> When you read a poem, see if you can clap out its rhythm with your hands.

See for yourself

Open up a book of poetry and choose a poem to read aloud. How does the poem's rhythm make you feel?

Rap songs often have a very strong rhythm or beat.

What Is a Stanza?

Some poems are divided into **stanzas**. A stanza is a group of lines that are separated from other lines in the poem by a space. A stanza is sometimes called a verse. Different types of stanzas have different names, depending on the number of lines in them.

Popular poems

Shel Silverstein (1930–1999) was an American writer who wrote a lot of poetry for children. He wrote poems in couplets, such as *Ticklish Tom*, and many other poems with different structures. Find some of Silverstein's poems. What do you notice about the stanzas he has used?

Shel Silverstein was also a songwriter and cartoonist.

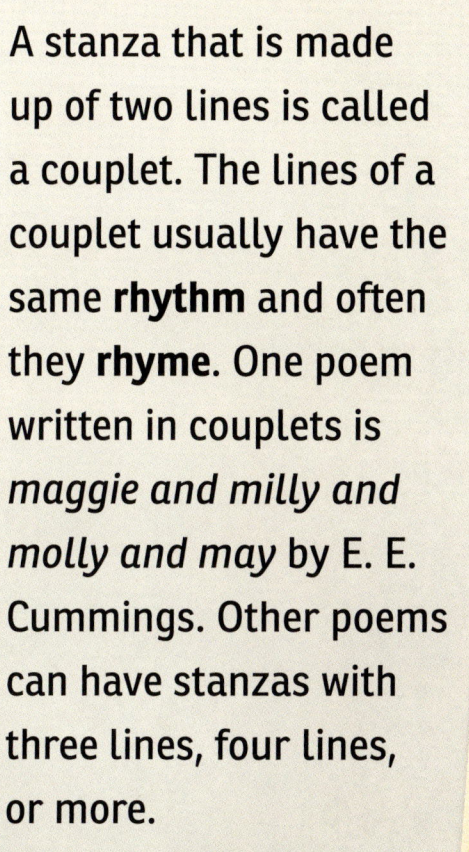

A stanza that is made up of two lines is called a couplet. The lines of a couplet usually have the same **rhythm** and often they **rhyme**. One poem written in couplets is *maggie and milly and molly and may* by E. E. Cummings. Other poems can have stanzas with three lines, four lines, or more.

The poem *The Tyger* by William Blake has stanzas with four lines.

Rhyming Patterns

If you flip through a book of poetry and read the poems aloud, you'll notice that many of them **rhyme**. When a poem rhymes, some of the lines end with the same sound—for example, "day" and "say."

When we look at the way rhyme works in a poem, we talk about the **rhyme scheme**. Poets can use different types of rhyme scheme in their work. Sometimes poetry is written in pairs of rhyming lines called **rhyming couplets**. For example:

> I shot an arrow into the **air**
> It fell to earth, I knew not **where**
> (Henry Wadsworth Longfellow)

Poet Henry Wadsworth Longfellow used rhyming couplets in his poem *Paul Revere's Ride*.

Popular poems

The **lyrics**, or words, to many pop songs rhyme. The repeated sounds we hear in the song help to make the words stick in our minds. If you find yourself singing along to a song on the radio, listen carefully and see if it rhymes.

The singer Adele has written many catchy songs.

Some poems are written so the rhymes come in alternate lines. For example:

> I remember, I remember
> The house where I was **born**,
> The little window where the sun
> Came peeping in at **morn**.
> (Thomas Hood)

Other poems may have more complicated rhyme schemes.

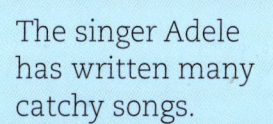

Using Sound in Poems

Poets choosing the words for a poem think about how they can affect as many of a reader's or listener's senses as possible. Good poets use the sounds of the words in wonderful ways to make us think or feel different things.

Here are some of the sound effects poets use:

Effect	How it works	Example
alliteration	words in a poem start with the same consonant	ghostly galleon wild whirling water
assonance	words have vowel sounds in them that sound the same	the mist swirled and curled around the house
onomatopoeia	words sound like the thing they are describing	"plop" sounds like the noise a stone makes when it plops into water

Popular poems

Look for the poem *Cynthia in the Snow* by Gwendolyn Brooks. Read it out loud. Do you think the words "shushes" and "hushes" sound like the sound your feet make as you trudge through snow?

Can you find any examples of alliteration in this poem by Robert Frost?

MOWING

There was never a sound beside wood but one,
And that was my long scythe whispering to the ground.
What was it it whispered? I knew not well myself;
Perhaps it was something about the heat of the sun,
Something, perhaps about the lack of sound—
And that was why it whispered and did not speak.
It was no dream of the gift of idle hours,
Or easy gold at the hand of fay or elf:
Anything more than the truth would have seemed too weak.
To the earnest love that laid the swale in rows,
Not without feeble-pointed spikes of flowers
(Pale orchises), and scared a bright green snake.
The fact is the sweetest dream that labor knows,
My long scythe whispered and left the hay to make.

What Is Free Verse?

Free verse is poetry that doesn't have any rules. Poems written in free verse don't have to be divided into **stanzas** or have a fixed **rhythm** or rhyming pattern. This type of poem can give poets a lot more freedom to express themselves in original ways.

When poets write free verse, they still pick every word very carefully to have a powerful effect on the reader. In addition to **alliteration**, **assonance**, and **onomatopoeia**, poets may also use other effects. For example:

Effect	How it works	Example
simile	compares one thing with another	as cold as ice fog like a blanket
metaphor	describes something as being another thing	his heart is ice the fog was a blanket

Popular poems

In the poem *Fog*, the poet Carl Sandburg uses a metaphor to describe the fog as a cat walking around. When poets describe things as if they are animals or people, it is called **personification**. Another example of this can be found in William Wordsworth's poem *Daffodils*, where he writes that the flowers are "tossing their heads in a sprightly dance."

You may sometimes write free verse in school.

Nursery Rhymes

A nursery rhyme is a traditional poem or song that has been around for hundreds of years. Some nursery rhymes are lullabies, with gentle **rhythms** to send a tired baby to sleep. Others tell stories, such as *Mary Had a Little Lamb*. They often have very strong rhythms and **rhymes** that make them easy to remember. For example:

> It's raining, it's pouring,
> The old man is snoring.
> He went to bed
> And bumped his head
> And couldn't get up in the morning.

SIMPLE SIMON

Simple Simon met a pieman
Going to the fair
Says Simple Simon to the pieman
Let me taste your ware

See for yourself

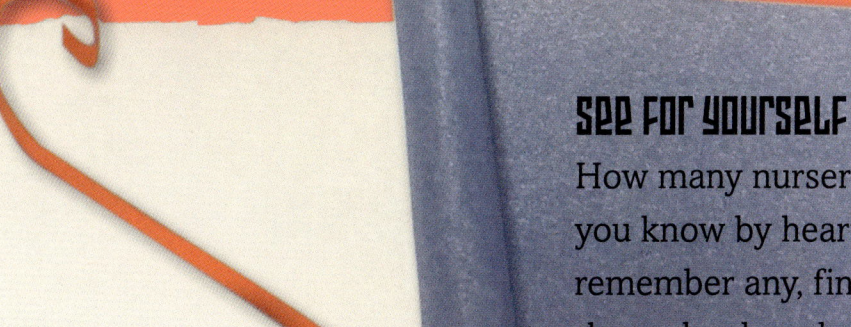

How many nursery rhymes do you know by heart? If you can't remember any, find a nursery rhyme book and see how many you recognize. What do you think helps us to remember these poems?

Many nursery rhymes include lots of repeated words or nonsense words. For example, in *Old MacDonald Had a Farm*, the sounds "e-i-e-i-o" are repeated, in addition to the animal noises. This makes the poem lots of fun to read or sing!

Some of the first poems we hear are nursery rhymes read to us by our parents.

Poems That Tell a Story

Many writers use a poem to tell a story. In the past, poets wrote epic poems that told long stories, often about heroes who go off on great adventures. Some examples are the ancient Greek epic poems *Iliad* and *Odyssey* and the Old English poem *Beowulf*.

The writer Roald Dahl wrote lots of funny story poems.

Popular poems

The English poet Alfred Tennyson wrote the poem *The Charge of the Light Brigade*. This poem describes what happens to a brigade of soldiers who ride bravely to fight a battle they have no hope of winning. It tells the story of a real-life event in a war when many soldiers died.

The poet Alfred Tennyson lived from 1809 to 1892.

Ballads are another type of poem that tell a story. Many ballads were originally sung to an audience. One very famous ballad is Samuel Taylor Coleridge's *The Rime of the Ancient Mariner*. This is the story of a ghostly sailor and his tale of a disastrous voyage.

Today, many poets tell stories in their poems. These poems may have a narrator and a range of characters. The poets have to tell the story in fewer words than in a novel or short story, so the language they choose is very important.

Funny Poems

Some of your favorite poems may be funny. Writers have used poems to make people laugh for thousands of years. Some funny poems have a fixed structure. A **limerick**, for example, always has five lines, with the first, second, and fifth lines rhyming, and a **rhyming couplet** on the third and fourth lines. Here is an example of a limerick by Edward Lear:

> There was a Young Lady whose chin
> Resembled the point of a pin;
> So she had it made sharp,
> And purchased a harp,
> And played several tunes with her chin.

Popular poems

Many modern children's poets write funny poems. Jack Prelutsky is an American poet who has written lots of famous funny poems, such as *I Made a Noise at School This Morning* and *Jellyfish Stew*.

Jack Prelutsky is a singer as well as a poet and often sets his poems to music.

Michael Rosen is a poet who writes and performs hilarious poems like *Chocolate Cake* and *The Itch*.

Edward Lear also wrote nonsense poems, such as *The Owl and the Pussycat*. Another poet, Hilaire Belloc, was well known for his **Cautionary Tales**. These poems tell the stories of children who have bad habits or don't listen to adults and meet a disastrous end. For example, a boy named Jim runs off at the zoo and is eaten by a lion!

Poems with Patterns

Some poems need to be read off the page because of the shapes and patterns they make. An **acrostic poem** is usually written so that if you read the first letter of each word downward, they spell out a new message or word. A list poem often repeats the same words at the start of each line. List poems often list lots of different information about something.

Popular poems

A **haiku** is a type of poem that was originally written in Japan. Haikus only have three lines. The first line has five **syllables**, the second line has seven syllables, and the last line has five syllables. Haikus describe a mood. Here is an example:

> Blowing from the west
> All the fallen leaves gather
> In the dark forest.

Jackie Kay's poem *Waves* is a list poem that can also be written out to look like waves on the sea.

Other poems may be written so that the lines make a shape or a picture that is linked to the meaning of the words. Sometimes these are called **calligrams**. The poet Gina Douthwaite has written many poems that make amazing shapes on the page, such as *Sweet Tooth*, and also *Do Not Disturb the Dinosaur*, where the whole poem is shaped like a dinosaur!

Performance Poetry

Some poets write performance poetry. These poems are specially written to be read out loud to an audience. When a performance poet performs, it is a bit like hearing music being performed. The poet is able to communicate directly with the audience and add to the effects of the language with the way he or she speaks and moves on the stage.

Linton Kwesi Johnson was born in Jamaica. He performs his poetry with Jamaican reggae music, which suits his style of verse.

The American poet Marc Smith invented the poetry slam.

Many performance poets want to communicate a message they feel strongly about, such as politics or the environment. They can reach people who would not normally pick up a book of poetry. Lots of new poets perform at **poetry slams**. This is when lots of poets read their work out loud and are judged by members of the audience. This can be very exciting for the poets and for the audience!

Write your own

Why not try writing your own poem to be performed in front of an audience? Think about something you care about. What do you want to tell people? Write a short poem and then perform it for your family and friends. Make sure you get their feedback.

Take It Further...

Start by picking up an **anthology** of poems written by different poets and flip through to see what appeals to you. If you find a poem you like, look out for more information about the poet and his or her work. What do you notice about each poem? Is it funny or does it tell a story? Can you spot any way the poet uses language to have an effect on you—for example, **onomatopoeia** or **alliteration**? When you've found some poems you like, try reading them out loud with your friends and family.

Allan Ahlberg has written many poems about life at school and other childhood experiences.

If you want more ideas to help you find poetry that appeals to you, you could try asking your teacher or a librarian. You might want to go to a poetry performance or slam and hear poetry being read. And, of course, you could try writing your own!

Ideas to get you started

Try writing a **limerick** that starts with this line:

"There once was a girl named Marie..."

Try writing a list poem about what you do on each day of the week. Try to include some alliteration if you can!

"On Monday I...
On Tuesday I..."

Write a poem that explains to your teacher why you haven't done your homework.

Glossary

acrostic poem poem in which the first letters of each word spell another word down the page

alliteration when words start with the same consonant

anthology collection of poems, often by different poets, in one book

artifact object made by humans

assonance when words have vowel sounds in them that sound the same

autobiography writer's own life story

biography someone else's life story

blurb text on the back cover of a book that briefly describes what the book is about

calligram poem that makes a picture when written down

cautionary tale poem or story that warns against bad habits or behavior

cross-hatching lines drawn over each other at different angles

empathize understand someone else's feelings

episode one section of a longer story

extended family other members of your family apart from your parents and siblings, such as grandparents, aunts, uncles, and cousins

fable story with a moral

feature part of a person or thing that stands out

fiction story that has been made up

first person when the narrator of a story talks about "I" or "we"

format style or layout of something

genre particular style of writing

haiku short poem, originally from Japan

ligne claire style of graphic novel illustration that has clear black outlines

limerick funny poem with a particular structure

lyrics words to a song

manga style of graphic novel illustration that started in Japan

metaphor when something is described as being another thing

myth very old, traditional story that is often about gods and the creation of the world

mythical found in myths

narrative account of events in a story

novel long story

observation something that the writer has noticed

onomatopoeia when words sound like the thing they are describing

past tense writing that describes events that have already happened

personification when something is described as if it is a person

plot storyline

poetry slam competition in which poets perform their work and are judged by an audience

present tense writing that describes events that are happening now

prose writing that is not poetry

protagonist main character

pun joke that uses words with more than one meaning

punch line final (and funniest) line of a joke

red herring information that is supposed to mislead the reader

rhyme when words have the same sounds

rhyme scheme way in which the lines of a poem rhyme

rhyming couplet pair of lines in a poem that rhyme

rhythm beat

setting place and time that a story takes place

shading adding of light and dark to a drawing

simile when one thing is compared with another

sonnet poem with 14 lines

stanza verse of a poem

storyboard sequence of sketches that show what will happen, and where, in a graphic novel

subplot less important strand of the story that happens alongside the main plot

suspense feeling of waiting for something exciting or scary to happen

syllable one sound within a word

third person when the narrator of a story talks about "her," "him," or "they"

Find Out More

Books

Novels

Kinney, Jeff. *The Wimpy Kid Do-It-Yourself Book*. New York: Amulet, 2011.

Stowell, Louie. *Write Your Own Story Book*. Tulsa, Okla.: EDC, 2011.

Warren, Celia. *How to Write Stories* (How to Write). Laguna Hills, Calif.: QEB, 2007.

Short stories

Johnson, Paul. *Get Writing!* Markham, Ont.: Pembroke, 2006.

Stowell, Louie. *Write Your Own Story Book*. Tulsa, Okla.: EDC, 2011.

Warren, Celia. *How to Write Stories* (How to Write). Laguna Hills, Calif.: QEB, 2007.

Graphic novels

Hamilton, John. *Graphic Novel* (You Write It!). Edina, Minn.: ABDO, 2009.

Lee, Frank. *How to Draw Your Own Graphic Novel*. New York: PowerKids, 2012.

Milbourne, Anna. *Drawing Cartoons* (Usborne Art Ideas). Tulsa, Okla.: EDC, 2003.

Poems

Magee, Wes. *How to Write Poems* (How to Write). Laguna Hills, Calif.: QEB, 2007.

Prelutsky, Jack. *Pizza, Pigs, and Poetry: How to Write a Poem*. New York: Greenwillow, 2008.

Raum, Elizabeth. *Poetry* (Culture in Action). Chicago: Raintree, 2010.

Web sites

Facthound offers a safe, fun way to find web sites related to this book. All the sites on Facthound have been researched by our staff.

Here's all you do:
Visit www.facthound.com
Type in this code: 9781410968319